DEC - 5 2007

DATE DUE

CROSS-SECTIONS
THE LCAC MILITARY HOVERCRAFT

by Steve Parker
illustrated by Alex Pang

Capstone
press

Mankato, Minnesota

Edge Books are published by Capstone Press, a Coughlan Publishing Company,
151 Good Counsel Drive, P.O. Box 669, Mankato, Minnesota 56002.
www.capstonepress.com

Library of Congress Cataloging-in-Publication Data
Parker, Steve.
    The LCAC military hovercraft/by Steve Parker; illustrated by Alex Pang.
    p. cm.—(Edge books. Cross-sections)
    Summary: "Provides an in-depth look at the LCAC military hovercraft, with
detailed cross-section diagrams, action photos, and fascinating facts"—Provided
by publisher.
    Includes bibliographical references and index.
    ISBN-13: 978-1-4296-0095-8 (hardcover)
    ISBN-10: 1-4296-0095-0 (hardcover)
    1. Landing craft—United States—Juvenile literature. 2. Ground-effect machines—
Juvenile literature. I. Title. II. Title: Landing Craft Air Cushioned military hovercraft.
V895.P28 2008
623.7'485—dc22   2007012862

Designed and produced by

David West 👫 Children's Books
7 Princeton Court
55 Felsham Road
Purney
London SW15 1AZ

Designer: Rob Shone
Editor: Gail Bushnell

Photo Credits
U.S. Navy, 1, 4–5, 7t, 7b, 10, 12, 14, 16–17, 18–19, 20, 22, 24, 25, 26; The
Hovercraft Museum, 6t; Ely Kumer, 6b; U.S. Marine Corps, 28–29; The Finnish
Defense Force, 29t; Ben Sheppard, 29b

TABLE OF CONTENTS

LANDING CRAFT AIR CUSHION

The LCAC is the U.S. military's hovercraft.
It launches from a large ship. Hovering
just above the water, it flies right onto the
beach. LCACs can even
land on other ships.

As a cargo carrier, the LCAC can deliver a massive load. The LCAC is used to transport troops, supplies, and even huge battle tanks.

Two propellers push the LCAC along over the waves. It roars right up onto the shore to deliver all kinds of cargo.

MILITARY HOVERCRAFT

Hovercraft are amphibious, meaning they can travel over water or land.

USEFUL INVENTION

The hovercraft was invented in 1956 by English radio engineer Christopher Cockerill. It is also called an Air Cushion Vehicle, or ACV. It rises above the surface on a down flow, or cushion, of air. Hovercraft are used worldwide to carry people and cargo across rivers, lakes, and seas.

The first full-sized test hovercraft, the SRN-1, made its initial flight in southern England on June 11, 1959.

Air cushion craft were used widely in the 1960s in the Vietnam conflict. The Bell PACV could cross jungle swamps and wide rivers.

Standard landing craft get as close to the beach as possible and then lower their ramps. But soldiers and vehicles still get wet as they travel ashore.

LCAC crews time their trips so that enough dry beach is uncovered by the tide.

A NEW WAY ONTO LAND

Military forces were quick to see the hovercraft's uses. This vehicle could be a new kind of landing craft. It would carry troops and equipment from huge transport ships to the dry ground of the shore. A hovercraft can travel over low rocks and reefs which would wreck regular boats.

FROM TEST TO PRODUCTION

During the 1970s, the United States tested two hovering landing craft, JEFF-A and JEFF-B. The B version was more successful. It was used as a basis to design the LCAC.

The U.S. Navy got its first LCAC in 1984. The craft passed its early tests. In 1987, full production started. The final LCAC was completed in 2001.

CROSS-SECTION

Some parts of the LCAC are named after those on ships. Other parts take their names from parts of airplanes.

The main body of the LCAC is known as the hull, as on a boat or ship. The front is the bow, and the rear is the stern. There are propellers like those found on a plane. The control station looks like the cockpit of an aircraft.

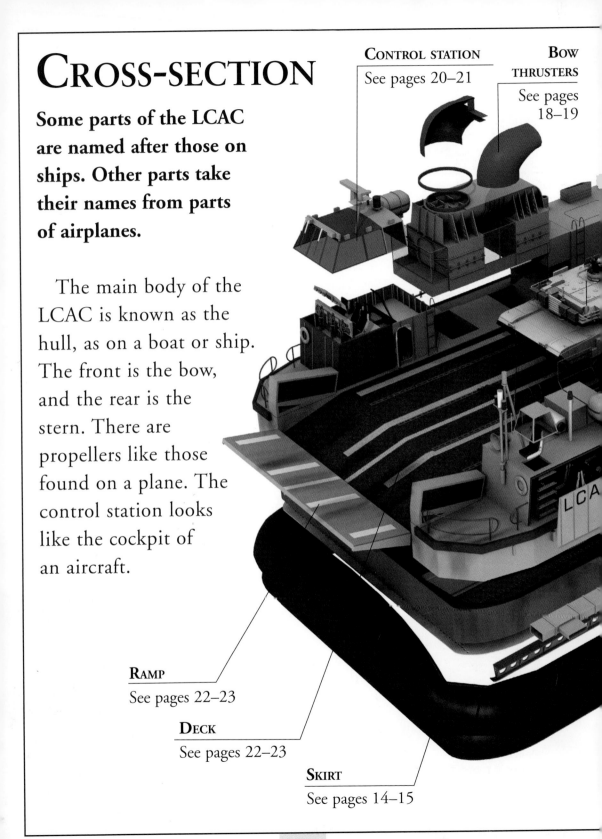

CONTROL STATION
See pages 20–21

BOW THRUSTERS
See pages 18–19

RAMP
See pages 22–23

DECK
See pages 22–23

SKIRT
See pages 14–15

ENGINES

See pages 10–11

RUDDERS

See pages 18–19

PROPELLERS

See pages 16–17

US NAVY

LANDING CRAFT AIR CUSHION
Length: 81 feet (24.7 meters);
87 feet, 11 inches (26.8
meters) with inflated skirt
Width: 43 feet, 7 inches (13.3
meters); 47 feet (14.3 meters)
with inflated skirt
Height: 19 feet, 6 inches (5.9
meters); 23 feet, 6 inches (7.2
meters) with inflated skirt
Weight: 87 tons (79 metric
tons) unloaded
Maximum speed: about 46
miles (74 kilometers) per
hour
Maximum load: 60 tons
(54 metric tons); 75 tons
(68 metric tons)
in overload
condition
Crew: 5

PAYLOAD

See pages 24–25

LIFT FANS

See pages 12–13

HULL

See pages 14–15

THE ENGINES

The LCAC has four engines that are all the same. They are known as marine gas turbines. Two drive the pusher propellers. The other two power the four lift fans.

A gas turbine works in a similar way to an airplane jet engine. Air is sucked in at the front, mixes with fuel, and is burned, or ignited. The burning exhaust gases blast out of the back. These gases spin fanlike turbine blades on the main drive shaft.

Fresh air swirls in through the side intake. Screens and filters keep out damaging sea spray, dust, and objects.

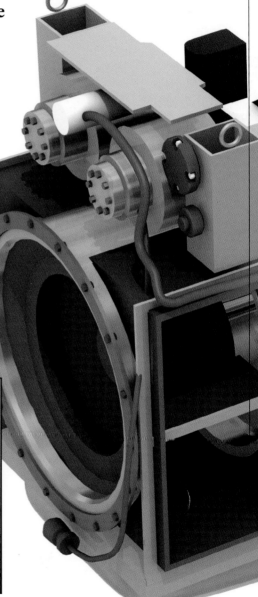

Two engines are enclosed in each side of the LCAC. They are cooled by fast-flowing air taken from the lift fans.

EXHAUST TURBINES

Four sets of angled turbine blades are fixed to the rear of the drive shaft. The burning exhaust gases push past them and make them turn the drive shaft.

Position of engines on the LCAC

DRIVE SHAFT

The drive shaft is spun by the exhaust turbines. It turns the LCAC's propellers and lift fans. The drive shaft also turns the turbine's impeller fan.

COMBUSTION CHAMBER

Inside the combustion chamber, the mixture of fuel and air burns continuously.

ENGINE SPECIFICATIONS

Four Avro Lycoming TF-40B gas turbines are each rated at 4,000 horsepower (hp). The upgrade includes 4 Vericor ETF-40B gas turbines at 4,745 hp each.

IMPELLER

This large intake fan strongly sucks in air. It makes the engine much more powerful than it would be with a natural inflow of air.

LIFT FANS

The LCAC's lift fans blast enough air out under the craft to lift the incredible weight of 200 tons (181 metric tons).

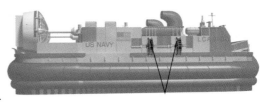

Position of lift fans on the LCAC

The front engine on each side of the LCAC drives a gearbox that spins the two lift fans in front of it. The fans are of the double-entry, double-outlet centrifugal type. They take in air through two inlets. As they spin fast, they push air down underneath the craft through two outlets.

LIFT FAN SHAFT

Power comes to the lift fan shaft through a gearbox. The gearbox slows down the turning speed of the engine.

AIR OUTLETS

The air flows into the duct system in the hull and down below the LCAC.

The huge air flow, or downdraft, from the lift fans makes water and sand spray up around the LCAC.

THRUSTER ROTATION MOTOR

An electric motor turns the bow thruster to direct the force of the air for steering.

BOW THRUSTER

This bent pipe carries air from the lift fans. The fast-moving air blows out powerfully and helps to steer and maneuver the craft.

LIFT FAN

The fan has curved blades. It measures 63 inches (1.6 meters) across.

FOREIGN OBJECT GUARD

A screen prevents large objects, including big seabirds, from being sucked into the lift fans.

HULL AND SKIRT

The hull, or main body, of the LCAC is one large, wide platform. The engines, lift fans, and other parts are in narrow housings along each side.

The skirt hangs down from the upper edge of the hull on all sides. It is made of canvas material treated with rubberlike chemicals. This design makes it flexible, airtight, and resistant to water.

The skirt blows up like a balloon as it traps air from the lift fans. The trapped air pushes down and lifts the LCAC hull about 4 feet (1.2 meters) above the surface.

The skirt bulges outward as air from the lift fans collects inside it and raises the air pressure. The air escapes through the fingers around the skirt base.

SKIRT
Creases and bulges lessen any stress points that might tear. The stiff makeup means the LCAC is less likely to wobble or bounce up and down.

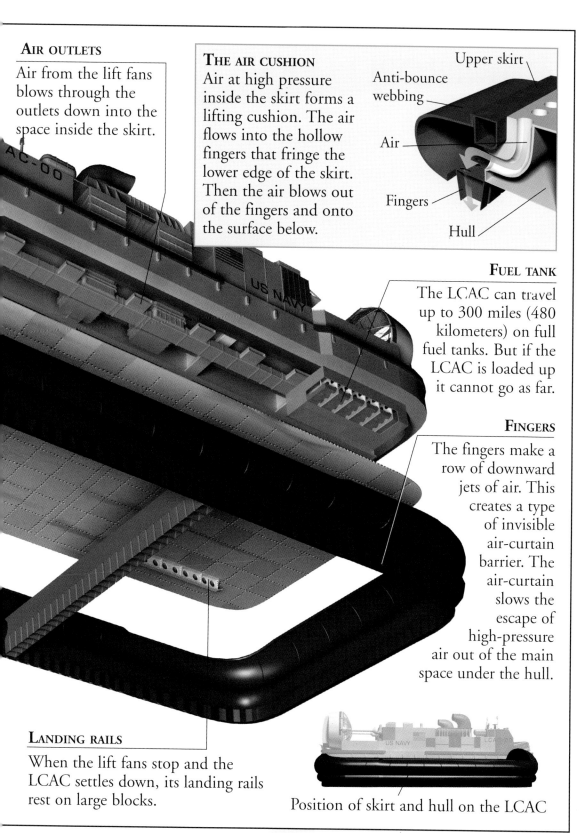

AIR OUTLETS

Air from the lift fans blows through the outlets down into the space inside the skirt.

THE AIR CUSHION

Air at high pressure inside the skirt forms a lifting cushion. The air flows into the hollow fingers that fringe the lower edge of the skirt. Then the air blows out of the fingers and onto the surface below.

Upper skirt

Anti-bounce webbing

Air

Fingers

Hull

FUEL TANK

The LCAC can travel up to 300 miles (480 kilometers) on full fuel tanks. But if the LCAC is loaded up it cannot go as far.

FINGERS

The fingers make a row of downward jets of air. This creates a type of invisible air-curtain barrier. The air-curtain slows the escape of high-pressure air out of the main space under the hull.

LANDING RAILS

When the lift fans stop and the LCAC settles down, its landing rails rest on large blocks.

Position of skirt and hull on the LCAC

THE PROPELLERS

The LCAC has two propellers at the rear, one port (on the left side) and one starboard (on the right side). They are airplane-type propellers with four blades.

A propeller is also called a screw, since it screws itself along, pulling whatever is attached to it. The blades have the shape of an airplane wing called an aerofoil. The shape makes the propeller suck air toward it, as well as blow air backward.

Like other parts of the LCAC, the Dowty R345 propellers must be specially made to resist corrosion. Corrosion is caused by salt and other chemicals in the sea water.

The blades of each propeller are made from extremely strong composite materials. Their rugged makeup reduces the need for repairs.

PROPELLER GUARD

This screen keeps objects from damaging the propeller. The objects bounce off the screen.

PROPELLER SHAFT

The propeller shaft is turned by the gas turbine engine in front of it. A gearbox reduces the turning speed of the engine for the propeller.

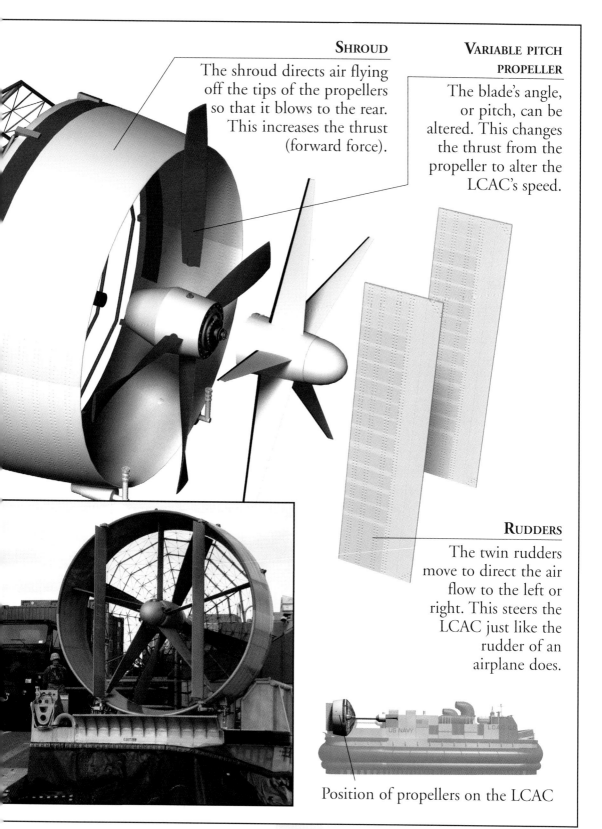

SHROUD

The shroud directs air flying off the tips of the propellers so that it blows to the rear. This increases the thrust (forward force).

VARIABLE PITCH PROPELLER

The blade's angle, or pitch, can be altered. This changes the thrust from the propeller to alter the LCAC's speed.

RUDDERS

The twin rudders move to direct the air flow to the left or right. This steers the LCAC just like the rudder of an airplane does.

Position of propellers on the LCAC

MANEUVERING

The LCAC flies over water and ground like a low-level airplane rather than traveling like a ship or land vehicle.

The LCAC is difficult to control. It does not grip the ground or cut through water, so it tends to drift and slide. It can be blown around by wind, pushed about by waves, and rocked unsteadily by both.

The main direction controls are the twin rudders on each propeller and the bow thrusters. Most maneuvers use a combination of these controls.

FORWARD

On a calm day with little wind, few waves, and weak tides, all controls can be set for straight ahead.

Force from bow thrusters

Cross wind

FORWARD
IN CROSS WIND

If there is wind from the side, the LCAC aims its bow thrusters to push the craft against the wind's direction. This keeps it going straight.

As the LCAC leaves its mother ship, it is suddenly exposed to waves and wind. The pilot must be extra alert at the controls.

AIRPLANE MOTION

Like a plane, the LCAC has three ways of moving. It goes forward or backward, steers from side to side, and lifts or lowers. It can also combine movements, such as leaning to one side or tipping nose-down.

CORNERING

The rudders swing to the right, forcing the propeller airflow to go at an angle. The rear then swings left and the craft steers to the right.

SIDEWAYS

At low speed, if the bow thrusters aim at right angles they push the whole craft sideways.

THE CONTROLS

The control station is a small room at the front right of the LCAC. It seats three crew members. The crew includes the craft navigator, the craft engineer, and the craft master.

The craft master is the onboard commander. He maneuvers the LCAC and gives out orders. The navigator plots the course, checks that the LCAC is heading in the correct direction, and looks for hazards. The engineer keeps an eye on the engines, fans, propellers, and other machinery. The engineer also controls the engine speed.

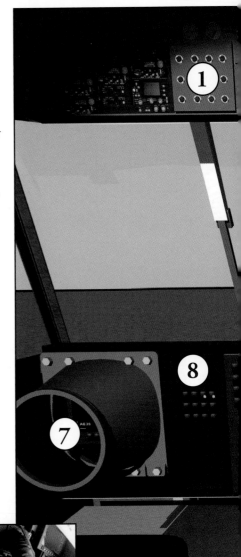

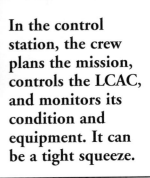

In the control station, the crew plans the mission, controls the LCAC, and monitors its condition and equipment. It can be a tight squeeze.

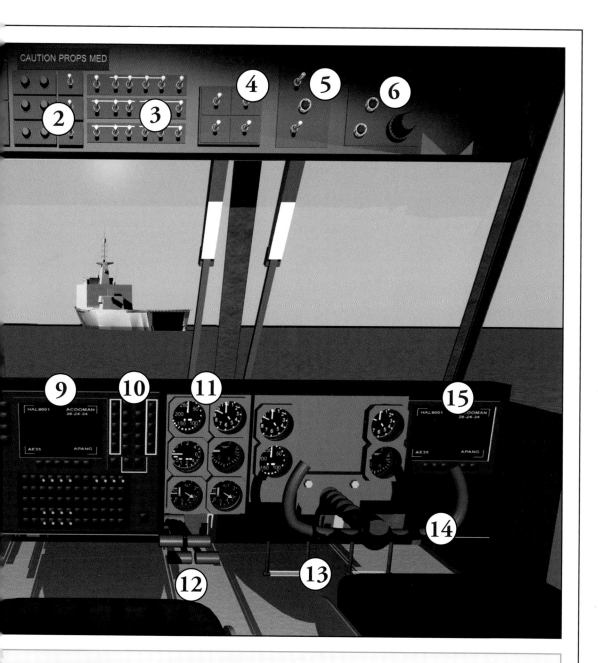

CAUTION PROPS MED

KEY TO COCKPIT CONTROLS

1. Radio communication controls
2. Engine balance switches
3. Engine starters
4. Windshield wiper controls
5. Ramp raise/lower
6. Air conditioning switch
7. Radar screen
8. Navigator's panel
9. Engineer's screen
10. Fire detection and extinguisher switches
11. Engine dials
12. Throttle (speed)
13. Rudder pedals
14. Steering yoke
15. Craft master's screen

DECK AND CREW

Other than the control station crew, there are two other crew members. These two crew members deal with loading and maintenance.

The load master decides where troops, vehicles, and other cargo should be positioned on the deck. He checks that everything is safe and secure, because the LCAC can buck and roll in big waves and high winds.

The deck engineer assists the craft engineer. He checks, maintains, and repairs the engines, lift fans, propellers, and other machinery.

CONTROL STATION

The high position gives a good view of the main deck and surroundings. The crew members talk to each other by intercom.

RADAR

The radar detects other objects in the area, such as ships and planes.

In the well deck of the mother ship, vehicles reverse onto the LCAC. To unload quickly, they drive straight off.

RAMP WINCH

The ramp is raised and lowered by strong cables that are wound onto winch reels.

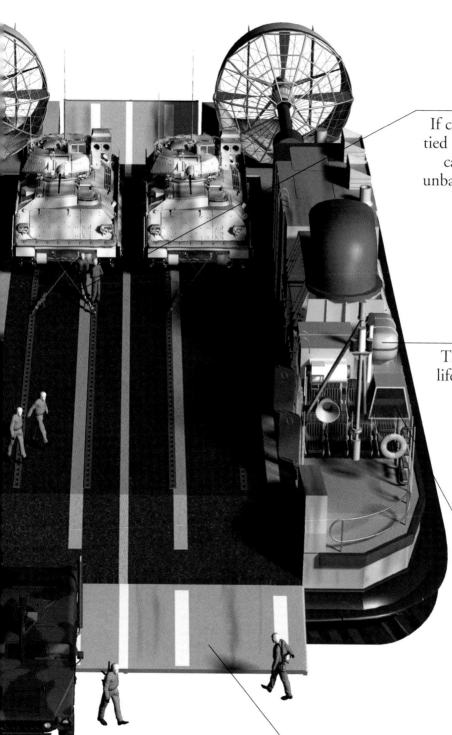

CARGO
TIEDOWN RAILS

If cargo is not firmly tied down, it can slip, cause damage, and unbalance the LCAC.

LIFEBOAT

The fully equipped lifeboat can be used in an emergency.

LOAD
MASTER'S
STATION

The load master plans the location of cargo so the LCAC stays balanced.

BOW RAMP

The main bow (front) ramp is 28 feet, 4 inches (8.6 meters) wide.

PAYLOADS

The LCAC can carry a load of 60 tons (54 metric tons). It can transport one M1 Abrams battle tank.

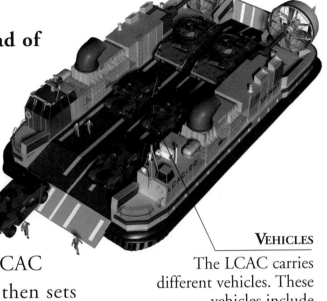

The LCAC loads in the well deck inside the mother ship. A full set of vehicles can be on the LCAC in 60 minutes. The LCAC then sets off for the shore. Unloading the LCAC takes as little as 30 minutes. One round trip, from ship to shore and back to ship, is called a sortie.

VEHICLES

The LCAC carries different vehicles. These vehicles include self-propelled guns such as the M109A6 Paladin. The LCAC also transports armored fighting vehicles such as M2 Bradleys.

An LCAC gets into position in the mother ship's well deck.

A tank moves slowly from the ramp onto the beach.

MAIN BATTLE TANK

A battle tank is close to the LCAC's weight limit. The load master positions it carefully to keep the LCAC stable.

TROOPS

The LCAC can carry up to 180 combat-ready troops. They may be in Personnel Transport Modules, or PTMs. These protective containers are assembled on the deck.

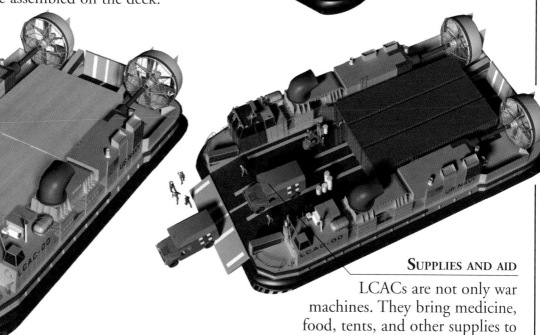

SUPPLIES AND AID

LCACs are not only war machines. They bring medicine, food, tents, and other supplies to areas hit by natural disasters like floods or earthquakes.

THE MISSION

LCACs can make much quicker, safer, and drier landings than standard landing craft.

The LCAC's air cushion means it can travel over water, low reefs, rocks, sand, mud, ice, and even marsh. The craft can access more than two-thirds of the world's shorelines. Boat-type landing craft can only access one-fifth of the shorelines. The LCAC clears obstacles 3 feet (1 meter) high. It has two machine guns for protection, and it can support heavier weapons systems for attack missions.

1. Fully loaded, LCACs leave the mother ship on a supply mission. The LCACs head to the landing area.

The order of landing is carefully planned. Troops get into position early, ready to counter an enemy attack on the LCAC.

2. A few LCACs drop their supplies high above the waterline and return for more.

3. One LCAC continues inland to reach a forward supply position.

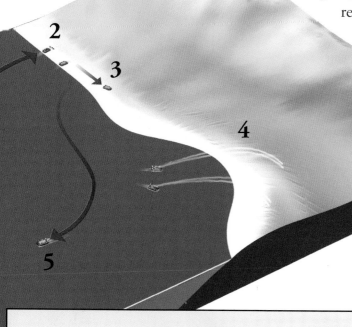

5. One LCAC is converted into a field hospital. It picks up wounded troops and races back to the ship.

4. Two LCACs fire explosives to clear a possible minefield. This makes the way safer for vehicles and troops.

THE FUTURE

There is no craft quite like the LCAC anywhere in the world. Since the 91st version was built in 2001, there are no plans to make any more. But many existing LCACs are being updated.

The Service Life Extension Program (SLEP) is a process of improving and updating older LCACs. SLEP includes new ETF-40B gas turbine engines. These engines have more power, use less fuel, and are easier to maintain. SLEP updates also include a deeper skirt to provide more lift. A more powerful and accurate radar system, known as the P-80, is also fitted during SLEP. LCACs that undergo SLEP have improved navigation equipment, better electronics, and stronger, longer-lasting hulls. All of these updates ensure that LCACs will be used until well after 2020.

The Expeditionary Fighting Vehicle (EFV) is a U.S. armored troop carrier. The EFV skims over water and has tracks for land. The EFV can do some of the same missions as the LCAC.

Finland's Tuuli hovercraft escorts its naval ships. It also protects Finnish civilian vessels such as fishing boats.

The Russian Zubr air cushion vehicle is similar to the LCAC but larger. It can carry 130 tons (118 metric tons) of cargo or 500 troops. That's more than twice the LCAC's payload.

GLOSSARY

amphibious (am-FIBB-ee-us)—a vehicle or craft that can travel over land and also over or in water

exhaust (eg-ZAWST)—very hot gases leaving an engine

gas turbine (GASS TUR-byne)—type of engine that works by hot gases spinning a turbine with fanlike blades

horsepower (HORSS-pou-ur)—the measurement of an engine's power, abbreviated hp

hull (HUL)—the main body or casing of a hovercraft, boat, ship, tank, or tanklike armored vehicle

mission (MIH-shuhn)—a task given to a person or group

radar (RAY-dar)—equipment that uses radio waves to find or guide objects

skirt (SKURT)—on a hovercraft, a flexible flap that hangs around the edges to trap air and create the air cushion

thrust (THRUHST)—the force that pushes a vehicle forward

READ MORE

Bullard, Lisa. *Hovercraft.* Pull Ahead Books. Minneapolis: Lerner, 2007.

Jackson, Kevin. *Discover the Hovercraft.* Germantown, Maryland: Flexitech LLC, 2004.

Sautter, Aaron. *Hovercrafts.* Horsepower. Mankato, Minn.: Capstone Press, 2007.

INTERNET SITES

FactHound offers a safe, fun way to find Internet sites related to this book. All of the sites on FactHound have been researched by our staff.

Here's how:
1. Visit *www.facthound.com*
2. Choose your grade level.
3. Type in this book ID **1429600950** for age-appropriate sites. You may also browse subjects by clicking on letters, or by clicking on pictures and words.
4. Click on the **Fetch It** button.

FactHound will fetch the best sites for you!

INDEX